Running a Profitable Small Business

Proven Advice from a Seasoned CFO

By Don Welker

RUNNING A PROFITABLE SMALL BUSINESS: PROVEN ADVICE FROM A SEASONED CFO

Don Welker/April, 2021

Dedication

I dedicate this book to my fiancée, Eva Garcia.

Acknowledgements

I would like to thank my editor, Linda Coss,
for helping me turn my vision into a reality.

Legal Disclaimer

CONTENTS

Introduction

"Many receive advice, only the wise profit by it."

~ Syrus

RUNNING A BUSINESS ISN'T EASY. In addition to ensuring that you have a high-quality product or service that meets market demands, and taking all of the steps necessary to market, sell and deliver this product or service, you must also stay on top of finances, ever-changing government regulations and labor laws, risk management and much more. Running a small business can be particularly challenging, because the limited number of people who are on your management team are each called upon to wear multiple hats.

As a CFO, I have over 30 years of experience working with a wide variety of businesses in a wide variety of situations. I understand the challenges that you face. It is my sincere hope that the advice presented in this book helps your small business avoid the pitfalls and achieve the success that you desire.

Chapter 1: Strategic Planning

"The essence of strategy is choosing what not to do."

~ Michael Porter

Avoid Growing Yourself Out of Business

QUITE OFTEN I TALK TO BUSINESSES that have big plans for growing sales, which is great. But what many business owners don't realize is that if you don't have adequate resources, that phenomenal sales growth can put you out of business.

Before you embark on a big new sales campaign, you first need to determine if you have the capacity to handle a significant increase in sales. For example:

- **Do you have the people in place to handle the anticipated increase?** A big increase in sales can impact every department of your company, from manufacturing, warehousing and shipping to accounting, marketing and administrative support. If your current staff is already operating at capacity, how will you handle the increased workload?

- **Do you have any idea how the increased sales will impact your expenses?** As you increase sales, you'll also increase your costs for raw materials, products purchased for resale, etc. But the increases don't stop there. Will you require more insurance coverage? Will you need to purchase equipment or hire more people? Will increasing head count mean that there are now more government regulations that you must meet? And so forth.

- **Do you have the credit in place to pay for this sales growth?** Most businesses have two types of credit: "financed credit," through banks or other lenders, and "unfinanced credit," meaning credit limits with suppliers. While I'll delve into this further in my next article, suffice it to say that as your sales and expenses grow, you'll have to expand your credit somehow in order to meet your increased cash flow needs.

- **Do you have the ability to meet increased reporting demands?** What I often see is that prior to a big increase in sales, the amount of credit that a company requires might keep them in one "rules category" with their lenders. Then they need more credit, and suddenly the bank wants to restructure the loan covenants and start seeing projections and monthly reporting on receivables. Creditors want to see the hard numbers that will make them feel comfortable that you're going to be able to repay them. Many organizations, especially those that do not have a CFO, do not have the capacity to produce these reports.

Growth is good – provided it is strategic growth for which you have planned. Skip the planning phase, though, and you run the risk of growing yourself out of business.

Budget for Growth

WHEN IT'S TIME TO BEGIN your annual budgeting process, do most of your team members want to run for the hills? If so, I've got good news for you. The budgeting process, including budgeting for growth, does not need to be a painful experience. In fact, if everyone arrives prepared, the process I'm going to describe here can usually be completed in two two-hour meetings.

Here's what you need to do:

- **Analyze your current level of business.** Before you can budget for growth you need to have a basic understanding of what's driving your current level of business, so that you can evaluate whether or not you can reasonably count on this level continuing.

- **Take a close look at your goals.** Your goals will drive your budgeting priorities. What changes need to happen in order for you to reach these goals? What additional resources (people, cash flow, machinery, etc.) will you need? Before you get too far, take a close look at whether achieving your desired growth goals would actually strengthen your company's financial position. As I discussed in a previous article, it's possible to grow yourself right out of business!

  For example, say your goal is to increase sales by 10% through a new contract with a big box store. In this case your sales volume would go up, but if the big box store squeezed you on price then your gross profit margin would go down. If they demand longer credit terms, you may have to borrow money to finance these new receivables. Add in the cost of any additional people you need to hire to service the business, and you might actually lose money on the deal.

- **Develop a plan of action and get 100% buy-in.** How will you obtain the necessary resources to reach your goals? What do you need to budget for, and who will be responsible for performing what?

As part of this step, be sure to assign some metrics to your goals so you'll be able to measure and report on performance.

- **Crank out the numbers.** Going through the above steps will give you a good foundation for a business plan. All that's left in the budget process is to decide how detailed you want your budget to be and calculate the numbers for each line item.

Budgeting does not need to take months...and even a minimalist approach can result in the solid plan you need.

Ensure Your Strategic Plan Will Work

HAVING A STRATEGIC PLAN in place for your business is the best way to ensure you achieve your goals. After all, if you're failing to plan, you're planning to fail. That said, it's not enough to create a strategic plan. You need to be sure that your strategic plan is created in a way that will increase its chances of success.

Be sure to:

- **Set obtainable goals** based on realistic projections, not wishful thinking.

- **Set realistic budgets** that cover actual costs and needs.

- **Create action plans** for implementing the strategies and tactics described in the strategic plan.

- **Get buy-in** from the people who will do or oversee the work.

- **Communicate the vision** and strategic objectives to the "rank and file" within the company and continue to communicate progress over time.

- **Assign responsibilities for each step**, including assigning due dates and timelines.

- **Plan for the infrastructure** needed to accomplish the goals laid out in the plan, such as:
  - People
  - Funds
  - Machinery
  - Physical space
  - Ability to obtain materials, parts or products
  - Production capacity
  - And more

- **Budget for mandated wage increases** caused by contractual obligations or increases in the minimum wage.

- **Do your homework**, such as to determine the actual viability of entering new markets.

- **Plan for proper marketing and sales support** for any new product launches.

- **Take steps to avoid scaring customers away** with poor customer service, negative press, etc.

- **Follow up at regular intervals** to ensure the plan is being implemented as anticipated.

Conduct an Annual Corporate Checkup

IF YOU'RE NOT CONDUCTING an annual corporate checkup, you're missing out on a significant opportunity to keep your business on track. What exactly is a corporate checkup? It's a chance to review what took place over the past year, take a hard look at actual versus plan, assess your company's overall health, and get ready to start planning for the next fiscal year.

How do you conduct a corporate checkup?

Schedule a meeting with senior management, including your company's CEO, COO, CFO and VP Marketing/Sales. Distribute copies of this year's strategic business plan (you do have an annual strategic business plan, right?), and have a frank discussion about the following:

- **Goals** – Did you achieve the goals that you laid out in your plan? Why or why not?

- **Implementation** – Did your implementation plan turn out to be workable and realistic? If not, what happened that you did not anticipate?

- **Unforeseen opportunities** – Did new, unforeseen opportunities arise? If so, did you succeed in taking advantage of them? Why or why not?

- **Employees** – Did you have the right employees to allow your company to succeed?

- **Working capital** – Did you have the necessary working capital to grow and thrive? Where do things stand now?

- **Vendors** – How strong were your relationships with your major vendors? Where do these relationships stand now?

- **Systems and processes** – How solid were your business processes and IT systems? Did any issues arise?

- **Financial reporting** – Were you able to provide formatted financial reports that everyone from senior management to outside lenders understood and had confidence in?

- **Financial dashboards** – Did you make use of weekly financial dashboards to manage your business more effectively?

The answers to these questions will help you assess the business' health and inform your strategic business plan for next year. In analyzing the answers, pay close attention to patterns in the things that the company seems to be doing right and areas in which you need to improve. What are the underlying causes of the problems you faced? For example, if you did not have the right employees, what areas did this impact?

Why is an annual corporate check-up so important?

Of course, since conducting an annual corporate check-up takes time and effort, you may be tempted to skip it. Don't give in to this temptation! This exercise gives the entire team a chance to step back, take a "big picture" look at what's been going on, and see things that aren't always obvious when you're enmeshed in the day-to-day challenge of running a business.

Chapter 2: Business Operations

"You can make a lot of mistakes and still recover if you run an efficient operation. Or you can be brilliant and still go out of business if you're too inefficient."

~ Sam Walton

Strengthen Your Customer Base

AS AN EXPERIENCED CFO, I know that some customers bring a lot more to your bottom line than others – and your biggest customers are often the least profitable. Which is why one of the things I do for my clients is to take a hard look at their customer base, analyze it and recommend ways to make it stronger. Here's how:

- **Analyze margins by customer.** How labor intensive is it to fill this customer's orders? How long does this customer typically take to pay? What is the average mark-up per order?

  Say you're in the fuel industry, and your truck can carry 8,000 gallons of fuel. Each delivery to the customer site incurs time and travel expenses. Your delivery cost per gallon will be much lower for the gas station that typically takes the full 8,000 gallons of fuel with each delivery than for the trucking company in the same neighborhood that takes only 2,000 gallons of fuel with each delivery. If the gas station usually pays their bill within seven days while the trucking company takes longer to pay, your margins will go down that much more.

- **Up-sell customers with higher-margin products.** For customers that want to buy a particular product as cheaply as possible, see if you can also add your higher-margin products to their orders, too.

- **Consider firing your largest volume customer.** Quite often your largest volume customer can be the one with the lowest margins. They can be the most labor-intensive to serve and the slowest to pay you. Plus, they often create the most stress in your office, because they have the most "fire drills." Take a hard look at whether or not this customer's business is worth it. Maybe it is. But maybe it's not.

- **Reduce customer-caused fire drills.** Before you fire a customer, though, look at ways that you can be more successful with them.

For example, what if your major customer often calls demanding that you drop everything to send a truck out because they just noticed they can't wait for their regularly-scheduled fuel delivery? Could you put an electronic monitor on their tank so that you can proactively serve their needs? Could you have the salesperson win over the person who's supposed to check the tanks? Could your CFO explain to their management that in exchange for great pricing, they need to reduce these "emergencies"?

Make the Most of Your Supplier Relationships

A WHILE BACK I WAS working for a firm in the oil business. We had an "exclusive vendor" supply contract with an independent petroleum refiner for certain service stations. We committed to ensuring that these service stations would purchase an agreed-upon amount of the refiner's gasoline over a five-year period, and that they would only purchase the refiner's brand gasoline. In exchange, the refiner covered the costs associated with branding these service stations and paid for a national advertising campaign for their brand of gasoline. It was a "win/win" for everyone involved.

Should you pursue exclusive relationships with your suppliers?

Many organizations find it beneficial to enter into exclusive vendor contracts whereby they agree to make a particular supplier their *only* supplier for a given set of products or services. The potential benefits include better prices, better service, marketing assistance and the ability to sell products that have brand recognition.

On the other hand, there is one major drawback: Exclusive vendor relationships make you dependent on one supplier, which always carries certain risks. As with any decision, you'll want to analyze the pros and cons of each particular situation before moving forward.

What can you do to nurture your supplier relationships?

What I see in the field is that most businesses know who their top five customers are, and place a lot of value in that. But they don't realize that it's just as important to recognize who their top five suppliers are, and value them in the same light.

Whether or not you have exclusive relationships with your suppliers, your vendor relationships are just as important as your relationships with your customers or your bank. Some of the best ways to nurture these relationships are to:

- **Be loyal.**

- **Provide adequate lead times.**

- **Pay your bills on time, and within the agreed-upon terms.**

- **Honor any volume-based purchase commitments.**

- **Be pleasant to work with and treat them fairly.**

- **Keep them informed about what's going on in your company.**

- **Communicate about any issues** that may be preventing you from honoring your commitments. For example, your needs have changed and your primary supplier is not offering what you need. Or maybe other suppliers are now offering better pricing. Give your primary vendor an opportunity to work things out with you.

Your vendor relationships are like partnerships. They want you to be successful so you can continue to buy from them. And you want them to do well so they can continue to meet your needs.

Improve Your Negotiating Skills

AS A CFO I'VE BEEN INVOLVED in many contract negotiations. Over the years I've seen what works and what does not. Want to increase the chances of a positive outcome in *your* next contract negotiation? Here is my advice:

- **Start the process early** – It always takes longer than you anticipate.

- **Be clear about your goals** – Before the negotiations begin, be sure your own team has reached a consensus regarding what your goals are, and where your drop-dead point is. Your overriding goal should be to have a contract that leaves everyone feeling good about the relationship while giving you the profit or ROI that you need.

- **Do your homework** – If you make a claim you must be able to support it. If, for example, you're saying that the direct cost of operating a warehouse is $X, then you'd better have a cost build-up that you can refer to when challenged (and you *will* be challenged!) to prove that this figure is real.

- **Negotiate in good faith** – And be honest. Honesty is always the best policy.

- **Be willing to compromise a little** – It must be a win/win, or at least a "face saving outcome," for everyone involved. I recently negotiated a cost-plus contract. When the representative of the other company realized he would have to go along with our proposal, he asked for something he "could take back to his people to show that he had won something." I said, "of course." Our long-term goal was to be able to renegotiate another contract with these people, and we had to leave the door open to that.

- **Consider including escalations** – You'll have to live with this agreement for the length of the contract. How will this affect you as costs change? Something doable now might not be doable three years from now if you have not worked in some escalations.

- **Keep your emotions out of it** – Always remember that this is a business deal. Don't make it personal.

- **Take detailed notes** – Type up your meeting minutes—including the details of any agreed-upon commitments—within 24 hours of the meeting, and then have all parties sign off on them. You'd be surprised how often people come away from a meeting with completely different understandings of exactly what was said.

- **Be careful what you put up on the board** – Never put anything up that you don't want someone taking a picture of. I've been in situations where the other side tried to claim they never suggested something...only to discover that we had photographic proof that they did.

- **Have all contracts reviewed by your attorney** – Never assume that the wording means what you think it means.

Put Appropriate Policies and Procedures in Place

WHEN A COMPANY IS first starting out, it is common for the owner/CEO to make nearly all of the decisions. But as a company grows, this approach becomes completely unworkable. Not only is it just too much for one person to tackle, it's really not the best use of the CEO's time. Delegating many of the day-to-day decisions to members of lower, middle and upper management becomes a must.

Why establish formal policies and procedures?

Delegation, of course, involves a certain level of risk. How do you ensure that decisions and approvals are made and given in a manner that is consistent with the goals and values of senior management—and in compliance with all applicable laws and regulations—without requiring senior management to be tied up with routine decisions? You establish policies and procedures.

Policies and procedures ensure consistency. They can mean the difference between order and chaos, and compliance and noncompliance. They can also save a great deal of time for everyone involved. After all, when everyone understands the guidelines, decision-making becomes easier.

Establishing appropriate policies and procedures

Depending on the nature of the business, there are a wide variety of policies and procedures to establish. These include:

- **Sales and pricing** – Determining minimum order size and minimum acceptable profit on an order

- **Extending credit** – Evaluating a potential customer's credit; issuing credit memos

- **Purchasing** – Creating purchase orders; opening accounts with new vendors; approving invoices for payment

- **Human resources** – Establishing employee pay rates and pay increases; allowing use of company vehicles and credit cards

- **Managerial approvals** – Approving expense reimbursements; authorizing corporate travel; signing checks

- **Legal** – Archiving and retaining everything from emails to contracts to financial records

- **Marketing** – Ensuring branding consistency; establishing who is allowed to publicly represent the company to the media

- **IT** – Creating an escalation system; requiring system documentation; ensuring backups take place

Communicating the policies and procedures

It is vital that the policies be written and available for people to see. This can mean putting things in print, uploading them to a corporate wiki, or using some other type of digital document sharing system. For some policies, such as HR-related policies, you'll want to give each employee a copy in writing and have them sign documentation stating that they're aware of and have reviewed the policies.

Avoid Unpleasant Surprises

IN BUSINESS, AS IN LIFE, there are "good" surprises and there are "bad" surprises. Winning an unexpected award is good. Discovering that you're not in compliance with an important regulation is not.

Over the years I've seen that many undesirable situations arise because of poor planning, inadequate oversight and controls, and so forth. For example:

- **Your reported earnings require significant downward adjustments.** This is often caused by under-accruing for vacation or holiday pay, bad debts, or your self-insurance reserve. This can happen when (a) someone is cooking the books, or (b) the person handling your financials does not have the expertise to get it right.

- **The value of your inventory is grossly overstated.** Sometimes this is caused by not having a reliable perpetual inventory system. In many industries, obsolescence is a big issue. Electronics that were fully sellable two years ago at full price may be fairly worthless now. Your financials need to reflect this.

- **Your strategic plan did not adequately plan for your growth.** Now you've got a huge order that you can't fulfill or you're sitting on the sidelines watching your competitors take advantage of new market opportunities that you can't, because you don't have the resources to do so.

- **You're blindsided by technical obsolescence issues.** You failed to plan for the fact that many aspects of your business can be affected by technological changes. For example, obsolete IT systems can become unreliable or inadequate, resulting in a significant negative impact on your operations. Your product and/or product delivery system can become obsolete. If you were selling music via CDs and didn't see the MP3s coming—or were relying on MP3s and didn't see the streaming paradigm coming—your sales would take quite a hit.

- **You're losing money on every sale.** You could be buying something for $110 and selling it for $105, thinking that you bought it at $90. How can this happen? Not issuing purchase orders can do it. A manufacturer that is using cost accounting standards can also incur this result. Quite often, your actual numbers for raw materials, labor, overhead, etc., turn out to be higher than the standards upon which your cost numbers are based.

Increase Your Cash Position

CASH FLOW PROBLEMS can derail your business. If you're running into cash flow problems, here are steps you can take to increase your cash position:

- **Speed up collections.** Take a close look at your accounts receivable aging report. Identify the slow pay customers and come up with a plan to address them. Perhaps you haven't been speaking to the right person, or your senior management needs to get involved by called their senior management.

  If you can afford it, consider offering customers discounts for early pay. While I don't generally recommend this, sometimes it's warranted if your margins are high enough. Of course, if you can afford it, the fastest but most expensive way to speed up collections is to factor your invoices.

- **Increase inventory turns.** Review your product line by item to get a good understanding of your sales by month, quarter and year. Take a look at your vendor's minimum order sizes and the delivery lead time for each item. Based on all this data, take steps to ensure you don't carry excess inventory.

  In addition, have a plan to get rid of slow moving or soon-to-be-obsolete items, and insist on having firm order commitments before bringing new products into your inventory.

- **Reduce your investment in fixed assets.** Review your utilization of existing fixed assets. Are there things that you're not really using that you could sell to generate some cash? For example, say you're a grading contractor. You have heavy equipment and a fleet of pickup trucks. Business has dropped 30%. You've already reduced your staff. Do you hang onto all that idle equipment for when business turns back around, or bite the bullet and liquidate it?

  In addition, I recommend that you avoid having an "always buy" mindset when investing in fixed assets. Sometimes leasing is best.

- **Negotiate payment terms that match your cash flow cycle.** If it typically takes 120 days from the time you purchase raw materials or inventory items to the time you collect payment from your customers, but your vendor expects payments in 30 days, your cash flow will quickly get out of whack. Talk to your vendor and see what kind of terms they can provide.

- **Obtain a working capital line of credit.** While there's a cost associated with this, a line of credit provides an immediate improvement in your cash position.

- **Develop and adhere to an honest operating budget.** Resist the urge to splurge on ego-related items such as an expensive company car, or to run personal expenses through the company account.

Ensure You Have an Adequate Accounting Staff

PITY THE POOR ACCOUNTING DEPARTMENT. When business is booming and everyone is high-fiving that sales went up 25%, management starts to think about hiring more production staff to handle the extra volume. But the impact of the extra sales volume on the accounting staff is often ignored.

However, when revenue drops off, the staff reductions often hit the accounting department first. With optimism running high that sales will get back on target, no one wants to cut sales, customer service or production staff. So the accounting team takes the hit...even though they still have a great deal of work (such as processing payroll and ensuring the lights stay on) that's not tied to sales volume at all.

Inadequate accounting staffing levels can hinder your company

Consequently, whether their company is growing or shrinking, many Controllers and Accounting Managers feel like they're just treading water. With staffing levels inadequate for the volume of work to be done, analysis and other high-level tasks take a back seat to keeping up with the basics, such as creating invoices and paying bills.

In situations like these, there's a lot that may be falling through the cracks. For example:

- **No one is looking at the likely impact of shrinking sales on projected cash flow, and how this will affect operations.** Will you run into a problem with your bank on your loan covenants? Will you be able to continue taking advantage of "early pay" discounts from your vendors? Will you make payroll?

- **Internal control processes are not being followed.** When something doesn't look quite right, no one is taking the time to investigate why the numbers are what they are. Or even worse, perhaps no one is taking the time to look at the numbers closely enough to even notice that they don't look right.

- **You're in danger of growing yourself out of business.** No one is looking at how increased sales volumes will affect your staffing and working capital needs.

The solution: Bring in a part-time CFO

A part-time CFO can help right-size your accounting department, working on an hourly or project basis to get all of those high-level accounting tasks handled. They can create and review the reports, do the analysis, provide oversight, help the Controller prioritize tasks, address projects that are important to senior management and much more.

Bring in Outside Professionals

BIG COMPANIES OFTEN HAVE big staffs and the ability to manage many things in-house. Small businesses and start-ups take advantage of the tremendous value that outsourced professionals bring. For a fraction of the cost of bringing a full-time employee on board you can have a highly experienced expert on your team.

Who should you be hiring? What I've seen is that most small- to medium-sized companies benefit from the services of the following:

- **Business Transaction Attorney** – Your business transaction attorney can help you form a corporate entity, and then ensure that this entity remains in compliance with board minutes, state filings, etc. on an on-going basis. Your attorney can also provide advice on day-to-day legal matters, such as contracts and regulatory compliance. When it comes to contracts, keep in mind that if *their* attorney wrote it, it's written in *their* best interests...not yours.

- **Tax Accountant** – Look for an experienced CPA who is familiar with your industry. Your tax accountant will provide tax planning and services and be available to help you with special projects as they arise.

- **Insurance Broker** – A good insurance broker will start by spending the time necessary to really understand your business and then create an appropriate risk mitigation plan for you. Your broker can obtain quotes from reputable carriers that understand your industry, and help you take advantage of the carrier's safety programs and discounts for best practices.

- **Banker** – Unless you have so much capital that cash flow is not an issue, your banker can be your business' lifeline to both fixed term and revolving working capital loans. A banker will also tailor your banking services to your company's needs, such as by providing remote check deposit services, zero balance accounts and more.

  Like the other professionals on your outsourced team, a good banker will take the time to know your business and its CEO and Senior Management Team. This enables your banker to tailor your loan covenants in a way that will help your business grow.

- **Part-Time CFO** – Much more than "just" a "numbers person," a CFO is a businessperson with many skills. Long before you have the need for a full-time CFO, you can bring in a part-timer (like me!) and start reaping the benefits of a CFO's expertise.

  Your part-time CFO can help you develop a strategic plan, review your finances to help you understand if you're adding value to your company, identify and eliminate wasteful spending and much more. This person can even help you assemble the rest of your outsourced team of seasoned pros!

Chapter 3:
Financial Management & Controls

"A budget is telling your money where to go instead of wondering where it went."

~ Dave Ramsey

Put These
Financial Controls in Place

ONE OF THE BIGGEST ACCOUNTING challenges faced by small businesses is caused by the fact that these organizations are small. When you're running a big corporation with a large accounting department, it's relatively easy to follow accounting best practices regarding separation of duties. But when very few people are involved with processing transactions, the business owner or a member of senior management needs to get involved with key aspects of the accounting process. This includes ensuring that a broad range of financial controls are in place.

Here are the financial controls that I believe are most important for small businesses to have:

- **Cash Management** – Bank reconciliations should be prepared on a monthly basis by someone other than the person who handles the banking, and then reviewed and approved by senior management. Companies that are victims of embezzlement schemes typically do not do monthly bank reconciliations at all, or do not have these documents properly reviewed.

  For money coming into the company, deposits should be made daily. For money going out, checks should be signed by owners or senior managers. The use of signature stamps should be eliminated or greatly minimized.

- **Purchasing** – Purchase Orders should be issued for all purchases. In addition, all new accounts with vendors or suppliers should be approved by the owner or a member of senior management. The person approving this account formation should also be responsible for informing the vendor that your company requires written purchase orders for all orders and providing the vendor with a list of personnel who are authorized to pick up purchases from Will Call.

- **Inventory** – When shipments arrive, the person who signs for the delivery should also note this receipt in the Receiving Log. While this is a very low-tech, "old school" tool, it is an excellent way to force the warehouse personnel to turn in the receiving paperwork. Of course, incoming shipments should only be accepted when they come with the proper paperwork. Similarly, outbound shipments should only be processed when they are accompanied by a delivery ticket or delivery receipt (which will become the customer's receiving documentation).

  Periodically completing a physical inventory is extremely important. Whether you do this once a month or once a year, you need to reconcile the physical inventory counts back to the balance in the account ledger to see if the variance is higher than what you'd expect with normal inventory shrinkage.

- **Accounts Payable** – When the accounts payable clerk goes to process an invoice for payment, he or she should match up the invoice with the purchase order and receiving document. Item descriptions, number, quantity and price should all be compared. The accounts payable clerk should indicate somewhere on the invoice that they have performed these steps and that they have approved the invoice for payment. Many organizations use a rubber stamp that has a spot for the person to initial to ensure this step takes place. If the invoice is for a service that does not create a receiving document, the invoice should be given to the head of the department responsible for ordering the service and they should indicate their approval on the invoice as well.

Once the checks have been printed, a list of all checks with the payees and amounts, along with the stack of approved invoices, should be given to the check signer. The check signer should be either the company owner or a member of senior management who is not involved with the rest of the accounts payable process.

- **Payroll** – Every time you hire a new employee you should have a profile sheet that shows who the person is, their rate of pay, assigned department, etc. Then someone other than the payroll clerk—preferably the owner or a member of senior management—should be the one to get the employee set up in the payroll system.

  When payroll is being processed, the owner or a member of senior management should review an input sheet or edit report to ensure accuracy. Take your time with this step, because it's a lot harder to fix the payroll after you push the "accept" or "send" button than before!

These are the most important financial controls for small businesses to have in place. If you address every item on this list you should be in pretty good shape.

Watch for Financial Control Warning Signs

I OFTEN SPEAK WITH BUSINESS OWNERS who thought they had appropriate cost and financial controls in place, only to be blindsided when they discover they do not. To avoid having this happen to you, too, watch out for the following. These are all warning signs that your financial controls might not be adequate for your needs:

- **You get an overdraft notice from your bank.** This is always bad news. The likely culprits include:

  - **Higher than expected labor costs,** which were not being properly tracked.
  - **Poor A/R collections,** with no controls to recognize problem accounts.
  - **Data entry errors** that made it look like you had more money in the account.
  - **Bank reconciliations** that are not taking place in a timely manner.

- **Inventory numbers in the system don't agree with the physical count.** While some minor variances are often to be expected, these numbers should never be significantly off.

In addition to theft, the likely culprits include:

  - **Data entry errors** – With no controls in place to catch them.

○ **Receiving shortages** – Instead of counting items when received, Receiving assumes the packing slip is correct.

○ **Shipping errors** – With no double-check that the correct items and quantities are being shipped.

▪ **Inventory values in the system don't reflect reality.** Instead of keeping a detailed perpetual inventory, some companies make the mistake of relying on gross profit percentages to track the value of inventory on hand.

For example, they assume a 35% gross profit margin on everything in category X. If they sell 1,000 items from category X for $1.00 each, they subtract $650 from the inventory account. But if the actual gross profit margin on some of these items is not 35%, the inventory values in the system will be incorrect.

▪ **Profits on completed jobs are lower than expected.** This is an indication that better financial controls are needed at every step of the job, from estimating through delivery. A weekly financial dashboard showing a snapshot of how the project is doing on key metrics, coupled with a monthly job cost schedule that drills down into the details, can be very helpful here.

▪ **You're paying for people who don't exist or time that wasn't worked.** This type of fraud is usually discovered when someone notices payroll is higher than expected. Ensuring you have a good time system and having someone in management other than the Controller review paychecks before they are distributed, can help avoid these situations.

Get a Handle on Your Month-End Close

IN ORDER TO PROPERLY MANAGE your company you need accurate and timely information. How are sales? Is your marketing program working? Are there any problems in operations? And so forth.

Underlying all of this, you need to have a firm grasp of your company's financials. For example...

- Are you on track to meet or exceed your goals, or do you have ground to make up?
- Is your spending proportionate to your sales level?
- Is your staffing level appropriate?
- Is your cash position getting stronger or weaker?
- Are you in compliance with your loan covenants?
- Is the information reported in your dashboard accurate?

Unfortunately, if you're struggling with your month-end close, chances are you're flying blind. You're making decisions based on inaccurate and outdated data, and don't have the necessary data to spot potentially problematic issues or trends before they get worse.

It's time to turn the situation around

If your month-end closes are not timely and accurate, you probably do not have the right team in place. To change this you need to be sure that your Accounting Department is staffed with people who have the training, time and skill set to ensure all of the following get done:

- **Basic accounting activities** – Including accurately completing billing, recording purchases and related accounts payable, processing payroll and maintaining up-to-date general ledger accounts.

- **General ledger analysis** – Completing a detailed review of the general ledger to identify and research any unusual or nonsensible entries or account balances. This function should be performed by a senior-level accountant.

- **Monthly financial statements** – Timely preparation of an accurate Balance Sheet, Income Statement and Statement of Cash Flow, all in a format that properly segregates current assets and liabilities from long-term assets and liabilities. This is usually done by the Controller or CFO.

- **Variance analysis** – A written narrative prepared by a strong Controller or CFO that clearly explains any significant variances from what was expected in the budget or plan, and what caused them to occur.

- **Compliance with loan covenants** – Failure to comply with loan covenants can ruin your banking relationship. Compliance with the reporting aspects of your loan covenants should be done by a strong Controller or the CFO as part of the monthly close process.

Be Aware of the
Most Common Types of Fraud

IT'S A RECURRING NIGHTMARE for many business owners. Something happens, and you suddenly discover that one of your trusted employees has been cheating you. Even worse, the fraudulent activity has been going on for quite some time.

The reality is, fraud can be very hard to detect. Here's why...

The Fraud: Overpaying for purchases

In this fraud the purchasing agent agrees to noncompetitive pricing, and then gets some type of kickback on every purchase, whether it's cash, travel or whatever. Even high-level employees can be on the take, such as a Controller or CFO responsible for professional services contracts.

- **Why this is hard to detect:** Quite often companies have complete faith in the person doing the purchasing. They do not require that this person gets competitive quotes on major areas of spending or have somebody review those quotes.

The Fraud: Phantom employees

What typically happens in this type of fraud is that somebody adds fictitious employees to the payroll. For example, a supervisor in the field submits paperwork for someone who doesn't exist, or for someone who exists but doesn't actually work for the company. HR has no idea it's a sham.

- **Why this is hard to detect:** Most companies will scrutinize time sheets but will not go out and physically verify that these people were on site during the stated dates and times. This can be especially challenging for companies with labor that fluctuates based on the workload. It can be easy for someone to submit falsified timecards for real people who were not actually employed by the firm at the time.

The Fraud: False overtime claims

This type of fraud generally requires collusion between the employee and the supervisor who approves their timecards. Often the employees are legitimately on the job on the days stated on the time sheet but are not actually working any overtime. The supervisor agrees to approve bogus overtime in return for a percentage of the extra pay.

- **Why this is hard to detect:** It is hard to detect a fraud that involves both the employee and the supervisor. To avoid this problem, a good control to put in place is a "labor budget." Supervisors must keep labor costs within this budget, with additional costs requiring additional approvals.

The Fraud: Embezzlement

What I've seen in this area is that someone in accounting opens up a bank account for a fictitious vendor, sets that vendor up in the A/P system and then cuts checks to them. While banking regulations make this harder than it used to be, it's still possible. Another common embezzlement scheme is to collude with a vendor who provides bills and receives checks, but who does not provide any actual goods or services.

- **Why this is hard to detect:** First, many companies do not have the necessary controls in place to prevent this type of problem, such as requiring the use of purchase orders, or requiring that multiple people approve new vendors. Second, once checks start regularly going out to a vendor, everyone becomes familiar with it. If a person can get away with the fraud for a few months, it's easy to keep it going.

Chapter 4:
Financial Reporting & Analysis

"As much as you need to know your operations, if you don't understand the finance side and how to do the business, you're never going to be successful."

~ Tilman J. Fertitta

Use Financial Dashboards

THE MONTHLY FINANCIAL REPORTS that most companies issue and review are a great way to keep tabs on how the business is doing. However, for most organizations, reviewing financial data once a month is really not frequent enough. If a problem is brewing, you might not see it until it's too late to change course.

Financial dashboards, which can be created on a project- or company-wide basis, fill in this gap. Usually set for weekly data, they give management a clear, high-level snapshot of current performance.

Your financial dashboard is used to track things that can be easily measured and converted into key metrics. While these metrics are most useful if you have a budget to which the numbers can be compared, they're still helpful even if you don't.

What to Include on a Company-Based Financial Dashboard

For a company-wide financial dashboard you might want to include the following metrics for that week:

- **A/R collections:** Actual versus budget

- **A/R aging:** Actual versus budget

- **A/P payments made:** Actual versus budget

- **A/P aging:** Actual versus budget

- **Payroll expense:** Actual versus budget

- **Full Time Equivalent (FTE) employees:** Actual versus last week and versus budget (useful for companies where labor fluctuates weekly)

- **Cash balances:** Actual versus last week and versus budget

What to Include on a Project-Based Dashboard

As this will vary greatly based on the industry, I'll present some possibilities for a construction firm. Here the idea is to track job progress by hours of work completed, and then support that by a measurement of where the project actually stands.

- **Actual labor hours**

- **% of project completed based on labor hours** (i.e. actual labor hours divided by total budgeted hours for the project)

- **Metric to measure work that was done**, actual versus plan. For example, if you're building a block wall, how many blocks were installed this week? How many blocks will there be in the entire wall?

- **% of project completed based on work actually done** (i.e. the metric that measures the work that was done divided by the metric representing the entire project)

- **Actual labor costs versus budgeted labor costs for this stage of the project.** If the project is 72% done, have you burned through more than 72% of the allotted labor budget?

Track Your Daily Production

IF YOU'RE RUNNING A MANUFACTURING or construction firm, it's important to know whether you're "winning" or "losing" from a production standpoint. How many units did you produce? How does this compare to your goal?

Ideally you should be tracking this every day. This way if things aren't going well, you've got time to take action before things get too far out of whack.

To track this information, I recommend using a daily key performance indicator (KPI) report card. Distributing this daily gives everyone from top management to your foremen and supervisors a clear understanding of where things stand.

Calculating your KPI goal

Of course, in order to determine your "units produced" KPI goal you need to first understand your fixed and variable costs. Knowing these lets you calculate your break-even point.

Let's do the math. If, for example, your fixed costs are $400,000/month and your gross profit is 20%/unit, your breakeven point is $2,000,000/month in sales. If your sales price is $200/unit, this translates to 10,000 units per month. On a simple 20-day month, this means your daily production KPI goal is 500 units.

Of course, most people don't go into business to just break even. Say you want to clear an operating profit of $200,000/month. Now you need to make and sell another 5,000 units/month (250 units/day), which makes your daily production KPI goal 750 units.

Matching your production goals to your workforce (and vice versa)

I believe that for most businesses the best way to approach this KPI is by looking at how many units you want to produce each day given the work force that you have. Why? Because typically most businesses are more successful if they can keep their workforce relatively static, rather than letting it fluctuate wildly based on variable production needs. This lets you avoid going into overtime mode because you don't have enough people, or end up with the expense of excess capacity.

Yes, reaching the ideal production level per man hours employed can be easier said than done, but it's certainly a worthy goal. And having a daily KPI report card can help get you there!

Make Your Financial Reports More User-Friendly

YOUR COMPANY'S FINANCIAL REPORTS provide the basis for a great deal of decision making. Unfortunately, many organizations distribute reports that are more confusing than enlightening—a situation that doesn't do anyone any good. To avoid this, here are some proven ways to make your financial reports easier to use:

- **Pay attention to formatting** – Just pushing a button in QuickBooks and spitting out a report often doesn't cut it. Take a few minutes to spruce up the formatting. This can make a big difference in a report's usability.

In addition to addressing the "look and feel" of the document, you also need to take a close look at the data that's being presented. Are there inconsistencies that you can eliminate? Are things presented in a logical order? For example, I've seen Income Statements that listed "labor" in six different places— none of which were at the top of the list, even though labor was the organization's number one cost.

- **Include narrative or context** – Chances are slim that everyone who reads the report will be able to instantly discern what the data is communicating. It is helpful to point out the key issues, and possibly provide a conclusion or suggestions for improvement. In many cases it is also a good idea to include historical or industry data, to give context to the data being presented.

- **Define all acronyms** – When sharing financial information it's important to speak English and not "accountant-ese." Don't assume everyone reading the report knows what "Cap Ex" or "EBITDA" is.

- **Provide a big-picture view** – In large companies it is common for the Income Statement to have 50 or more potential line items. Obviously, the report can get confusing if all 50 are included. It's just too much detail! In cases like this, see if you can consolidate things on the main report, and then offer the ability to drill down into the details as needed.

- **Tailor the report to the audience** – Think about who the report is for and customize it accordingly. Your rank-and-file employees, for instance, will be interested in different data than your investors and bankers, who may have different data needs than your executive team.

The bottom line is, if you're going to do the work to gather and analyze the data, put in the extra 10% more time to polish the report and make it more user-friendly. Confusing reports do not benefit anyone!

Make Your Chart of Accounts Work for You

YOUR CHART OF ACCOUNTS can be an important tool to help you monitor your business and make intelligent decisions. Or not. It all depends on how things are set up.

The "generic accounts setup" should just be a starting point

Every business' Chart of Accounts will include some of the same general accounts, such as cash, accounts receivable, assets, equity (hopefully), accounts payable, income, expenses, cost of goods sold (COGS), payroll taxes, etc.

However, I recommend that businesses never operate with just a generic Chart of Accounts, particularly when it comes to income and expenses. To really make your Chart of Accounts work for you, take the time to set up the accounts that are specific to your industry and how you want to monitor and manage your business.

What exactly would you like to be able to track and analyze? What level of granularity will help you determine how different aspects of your business are really doing? You need accounts that track this.

Example: Structural Concrete Contractor

Say you're running a construction contracting business specializing in structural concrete services. To set up your Chart of Accounts, start with the "generic" recommendations for construction contractors and then customize from there. Some of the things you may want to track include:

- **Labor costs by pay category** – To give you an understanding of your regular time pay, overtime pay and fringe benefits costs.

- **Materials expenses by material type** – Ideally your Chart of Accounts will mirror the details in the "Schedule of Values" (i.e. a breakdown of what it will cost to complete the job) that you use to create your bids.

  In other words, don't just lump rebar, concrete, wood and other materials into one "materials" account. If you do, then if you go over on materials, figuring out why will take a lot of work. Tracking materials expenses based on the same line items that are on the Schedule of Values lets you easily make an item-by-item comparison of actual to plan and quickly pinpoint the problem area.

  Having this information available is helpful even if you don't have any overages. When you're three months into a six-month project, this data will help you determine where you stand.

- **Indirect costs** – Think about how indirect costs impact how you want to track the performance of the job and set the accounts up accordingly.

Conduct an Effective Year-End Financial Review

WHEN I MEET WITH SMALL BUSINESS OWNERS, it often becomes clear that they are mystified by their business' financial statements. Unfortunately, because they don't know what to look for when evaluating these essential documents, they miss out on both red flags and opportunities.

In this 3-part tip I'll teach you how to evaluate the three parts of a quality set of year-end financial statements: Statement of Cash Flows, Income Statement and Balance Sheet.

STATEMENT OF CASH FLOWS

Cash is king

Because cash is so important, the Statement of Cash Flows is the first thing you should look at when conducting a year-end financial review. After all, when it comes to running and expanding a business, cash (or, more specifically, cash flow) truly is king.

Your Statement of Cash Flows helps answer some vital questions. Does your organization have enough cash to stay in business? Is it generating more cash than it's using—or vice versa?

Would it qualify for a bank loan? And more.

Start with the details

Your starting point should be to ask some important questions about the details:

- **How was cash generated by and used in operations?** For example, have your collections of trade receivables sped up or slowed down?

- **How was cash generated by and used in investing activities?** For example, did the company buy or sell property and/or equipment?

- **How was cash generated by and used in financing activities?** Did the company obtain cash through borrowing? Did it use cash to pay down lines of credit or other long-term debt?

Then look at the big picture

Next look at everything as a whole. Identify any non-cash expenses on your Statement of Cash Flows, such as amortization and depreciation. Add these back to your net income to help you get an accurate picture of your actual cash flow.

Compare cash at the beginning of the period to cash at the end of the period to see if your company is generating positive cash flow. Although there are some exceptions to the rule (such as start-up companies that have received an infusion of cash), generally speaking, if your company is generating positive cash flow then it is profitable. Which, of course, is what you're hoping to see.

INCOME STATEMENT

Whether you're reviewing your own company's financial statements or you're looking at another company's information, such as the financial statements for a customer that has applied for credit, it pays to know what to look for.

Start with some helpful comparisons

When evaluating an Income Statement, a good starting point is to compare the year-end Income Statement to that of the prior year. If you're reviewing your own company's financials, you should also compare it to budget.

Here are some of the first things you should look at:

- **Is the revenue going up or down?**

- **Are the gross profit margins increasing, decreasing or flat?**

- **Are operating expenses moving as you would expect** based on the changes in revenue?

- **How did actual performance compare with the budget forecast?**

Understand what happened during the year

Reviewing an Income Statement is not just a matter of seeing if the numbers look "about right" and moving on. You also need to ask questions to understand what happened during that time period. These include:

- **What's driving the change** (or lack of change) in gross profit margins?

- **If operating expenses are not moving in tandem with revenue,** why not? If expenses are rapidly accelerating, what's driving it? If cost-cutting measures slashed expenses, how are these measures affecting operations?

- **Were there any unusual or non-recurring expenses?** How would the Income Statement look if you pulled the one-time expenses out of the picture?

Be sure to look forward, too

Next you want to ask about how the events of the past year will likely impact the company going forward. For example:

- **Is it anticipated that the current levels** of revenues, operating expenses and gross profits will continue in each of the next four quarters? Why or why not?

- **Are the needed credit facilities in place** to support operations and/or anticipated growth? As I have discussed in a previous chapter, you need to avoid growing yourself out of business.

- **How are vendor relations?** Are there any potential supply issues that could affect operations?

I also like to ask divisional managers what two things could be changed in company operations to increase bottom-line profit. The answers can be very revealing!

BALANCE SHEET

Your Balance Sheet provides a snapshot of your business' financial condition at a specific moment in time—in this case, your fiscal year-end. It shows your firm's assets, liabilities and owners' or stockholders' equity.

Compare to last year

Just like when evaluating your Income Statement, your starting point in understanding the picture that your Balance Sheet is painting about your business is to compare it to the prior year. Take a close look at:

- **Cash** – Did cash go up or down? Do the numbers match what's on your Statement of Cash Flows? If not, an accounting error has been made somewhere—most likely in the Statement of Cash Flows, which can be tricky to compile.

- **Working Capital** – Working capital is your current assets minus your current liabilities. Is it positive or negative? Did it increase or decrease as compared to last year?

Look at important ratios

Next there are two important ratios that you should review:

- **Current Ratio** – The Current Ratio is the ratio of current assets to current liabilities. This provides an indication of your company's liquidity and ability to pay back its liabilities.

  Ideally, the Current Ratio will be stronger than 2:1. A ratio of 1:1 indicates that your company barely has the ability to meet its anticipated debts for the next 12 months. A ratio of less than 1:1 is usually a sign that your company is not in good financial health.

- **Leverage Ratio** – The "Leverage Ratio" is the ratio of debt to equity. Banks look at this ratio when deciding whether or not to approve a loan.

  A ratio of 4:1 or above is considered highly leveraged.

  A ratio of 2:1 or less is ideal. This indicates that your company has the ability to safely borrow additional debt.

  A ratio of 2.5:1 or 3:1 is in the upper limits of most banks' "safe zone." Borrowing money at this point is possible but more difficult.

Chapter 5:
Business Credit & Loans

*"If you would know the value of money,
go and try to borrow some."*

~ Benjamin Franklin

Ensure You Can Finance Growth

MANY BUSINESSES MAKE BIG PLANS for growing sales without making corresponding plans for growing capacity. You can push your people to work longer hours. You can bring in a part-time CFO such as me to handle your increased reporting needs and create a financial dashboard that will let you track things to ensure you're actually making money. But unless you've got a lot of cash, without adequate credit to finance your business expansion, your business is not going to expand.

For example, say your construction company is planning to grow by 30% over the next 12 months. You typically get 90% of the progress payment within 60 days and the remaining 10% remains as retention to be paid when the job has been completed by all trades. To accommodate your increase in sales your payroll will go up. But until the retention payments start to roll in, where is that money going to come from?

Or perhaps you have a manufacturing company with a 90-day production cycle. How will you pay for 30% more raw materials if you won't receive payment until 30 to 60 days after the product ships?

You need a strategic plan

To address this issue, start by determining exactly how much credit you're going to need. Your strategic business plan should address this by looking at how your sales increase will impact your anticipated cash flow and each of your expenses.

Look at your financed and unfinanced credit

Do you have unused credit that you can tap now? Are your suppliers willing to work with you to fill the gap? After all, if your suppliers are comfortable increasing your credit and continuing with your current terms, you're set. But if this is not the case, you'll need to work on expanding your financed lines of credit.

Give your lender the information they need

Before a bank or other lender will increase your line of credit, they'll want to see believable projections showing what your company will do in the next 12 to 36 months. Getting loan approval often depends on getting this aspect of your loan package right.

Get Your Loan Package Ready for the Spotlight

IT'S A FACT: LENDERS ONLY FUND LOANS when they're comfortable that they'll be able to collect both the principal they lend and the interest they charge. The degree of comfort they feel dictates how much they'll lend and the interest rate they'll charge. Your loan package must convince them that your request meets their criteria. Which is why getting it right is so crucial!

The key elements of a successful loan package

If you can provide the following items in a way that will make the lender agree the loan makes sense, you'll be able to secure the loan at a reasonable interest rate, with payment terms and loan covenants that you can safely satisfy. But if you're missing any of these elements, or if they don't point to your ability to repay the loan, then you're not likely to have much luck obtaining funding at all.

- **Business plan & projected financials** – You can help yourself get the best loan by having a solid business plan that forecasts revenue and expenses for the desired loan period. This plan must show where your company has been and where it is going in terms of sales growth, business opportunities and more.

  Your projected Profit & Loss Statement, Balance Sheet and Statement of Cash Flows provide the numbers that support your plan. Each of these financial statements should be presented on a quarterly basis for each quarter of the desired loan period.

- **Current financials** – In addition to the projections, lenders also want to see your current year's financials, which serve as a benchmark.

- **Narrative** – Your loan package must clearly show why you need the money, and when and how it will be paid back. While the numbers should do much of the "talking," if you don't already have a relationship with the lender it's best to include a page or two that lays out the assumptions and provides a top-level view of your company and plans.

- **Extra explanations** – In addition, be sure to provide more information for anything that might be a potential red flag. For example, if you're projecting 25% revenue growth in an industry that's flat, you need to explain how you will make this happen.

Getting the loan package right is crucial. If your internal finance people are not experienced with this, you'll want to bring in outside talent that is.

Know What Bankers Look for In a Business Plan

HAVING AN EXCELLENT LOAN PACKAGE is critical for convincing lenders that you are credit-worthy, and one of the key elements of a successful loan package is the business plan. Your business plan shows where your company has been and where it is going in terms of sales growth, business opportunities and more. Here's what that plan needs to include:

- **Business description** – A few paragraphs that explain what you do, including a brief description of your key products and services, an overview of your industry, and a sentence or two about each of the key members of your management team.

- **Historical financials** – Three years of historical financials (Profit & Loss Statement, Balance Sheet and Statement of Cash Flows).

- **High-level sales/marketing plan** – This needs to include a detailed 3- to 5-year sales forecast by major product lines showing projected sales units, and average sales price, costs and gross profit per unit sold...and narrative that explains how you'll make it happen.

  How does your projected growth compare to your industry's projected growth? How will you achieve your projected sales growth? For example, do you plan to introduce new products, find new markets for existing products, implement new processes that will improve profitability or what?

What actions will you take to support the projected sales volume? How will this sales volume impact your working capital requirements, staffing, production capacity, vendor relationships and other infrastructure issues?

- **Projected financials** – Three to five years (depending on the desired loan length) of projected financials based on this sales/marketing plan, all presented on a quarterly basis for each year. In addition to the Profit & Loss Statement and Balance Sheet, this includes:

  o **Operating expenses** with labor build-ups by department. If you're saying that you'll have four years of 8% year-over-year growth, what type of staffing will you need to support it?

  o **Debt and debt payments** needed to support this growth.

  o **Capital expense budget** outlining projected capital expenditures by year.

  o **Statement of Cash Flows** that ties all of this together.

Get a Loan
Without a Personal Guarantee

WISH YOU COULD GET A LOAN for your business without providing a personal guarantee? Join the club! Most business owners prefer not to put their personal assets on the line in this way. Banks, on the other hand, only want to lend when they're 100% comfortable that they will be able to get their money back—and a personal guarantee helps provide that reassurance.

Although it can be next to impossible for new companies to get loans without personal guarantees, established companies sometimes can. From what I've seen, here's what it takes:

- **Longevity** – Minimum of five years in business, but probably more than 10.

- **Profitability** – A track record of profitability and a demonstrated commitment to using these profits to grow the financial strength of your company.

- **Strong balance sheet** – Including:

  - **Quick Ratio** (cash plus accounts receivables, divided by current liabilities) of 2:1 or better

  - **Debt to Equity Ratio** of less than 1.0:1

- **Collateral** – This must be in excess of what you wish to borrow, with the bulk being liquid, such as cash or receivables. Lenders might also be interested in the real tangible value of inventory, machinery and equipment in a liquidation scenario.

- **Ability to repay** – Lenders want to see a realistic business forecast for the term of the loan showing that your business can easily meet the loan's debt service requirements.

- **Past loans** – A history of satisfying past loan obligations in a timely manner and remaining in full compliance with the loan covenants until the loans are repaid.

- **Prompt accounts payables** – Demonstrated history of paying your bills in a timely manner, as supported by consistent accounts payable aging with no past due balances.

- **Strong management** – A solid and consistent management team that doesn't change from year to year.

- **Long-term relationships** – Banks want to see that you cultivate and value long-term business relationships, that you're not changing banks, insurance brokers, CPAs or other professional service providers every year.

Finally, lenders want to know *why* you don't want to provide the personal guarantee. After all, if you're not comfortable providing this, why should they be comfortable putting their money into your business? A good first step might be to seek a reduced personal guarantee based upon mutually-agreed-upon metrics between you and the bank.

Avoid Ruining Your Banking Relationship

WHETHER YOUR COMPANY IS IN GROWTH MODE or trying to deal with flat or diminishing sales, there's a good chance you depend on credit from your bank to help you pay the bills. Which is why I'm always surprised to see how many companies do things that ruin their banking relationship!

Bankers are generally very cautious people. They need to feel completely confident that the money they loan to you will indeed be paid back. Do one of the following actions, and run the risk ruining your banking relationship:

- **Provide misinformation or no information** – The quickest way to lose your credit is to surprise your bankers. The worst way is to lie to them. If your company is struggling, the best time to tell your banker that there's a problem is as soon as you become aware of it.

- **Add to your debt** – In most cases, borrowing money from other sources (outside of trade payables) without your banker's approval or consent will violate your loan covenants.

- **Break the law** – Your banker will not be happy if you incur a significant regulatory violation by failing to comply with a law, such as not reporting or properly resolving a hazardous spill, or getting slapped with a class action lawsuit because you didn't comply with labor laws.

- **Miss your previously reported earnings projections** – Say your bank has raised a concern about your repeated failure to hit your leverage ratio, and you have assured them that this quarter you'll hit the numbers. If you don't, they might get "lender's fatigue" and give up on you.

- **Use corporate assets to buy luxury items** – If your banker sees that, while you're seeking to continue to expand your loan base, you're using corporate funds to buy luxury boats, planes or cars, they'll think twice about approving another loan.

- **Miss reporting deadlines** – It is vitally important that you provide accurate and timely financial statements and be proactive about telling your banker if something is amiss.

Most of the things on this list are typically covenant violations. Always keep in mind that your banker has the right to call your loan—and demand immediate payment—for *any* covenant violation, regardless of its magnitude. When that happens, I can tell you that it's really not a pleasant position to be in.

Chapter 6:
Insurance

"You can never protect yourself 100%.
What you do is protect yourself as much as possible
and mitigate risk to an acceptable degree."

~ Kevin Mitnick

Ensure You Have the Right Insurance in Place

LAWSUITS … FIRES … THEFT … FRAUD … injuries … cyberattacks … workers comp claims. Without careful planning, one disaster can destroy your business. To ensure that your business is protected, you must have the right types of insurance in place, with policies that offer adequate coverage levels for your needs.

Insurance policies that most businesses should consider

Not sure what you need? A good place to start is to talk to your insurance broker about:

- **Property and General Liability Insurance** – A must, this protects your property against physical damage and your company against claims of bodily injury or property damage.

- **Workers' Compensation Insurance** – Required in California if you have one or more employees.

- **Vehicle Insurance** – Mandatory if your company owns and operates any motor vehicles.

- **Health Insurance** – As of this writing, this is mandatory for companies of a certain size.

- **Directors and Officers Insurance (D&O)** – Protects your corporation's directors and officers from personal liability in the event of a claim against the business.

- **Key Person Life Insurance** – Can be important if your business depends on the knowledge or expertise of a particular person.

- **Employment Practices Liability Insurance** – Provides coverage against employment-related claims, such as discrimination, harassment or wrongful termination.

- **Business Interruption Insurance** – Covers the loss of income that your business suffers after a disaster.

- **Cybersecurity Insurance** – Helps address the damage after cyberattacks and data breaches.

Industry-specific insurance needs

Your business may also require industry-specific insurance coverage. Examples include:

- **Petroleum industry** – Environmental coverage in case there's a spill.

- **Construction industry** – Policies to fulfill bonding requirements.

- **Manufacturing industry** – Product liability insurance.

- **Professional services firms** – Errors & Omissions Insurance (also known as Professional Liability Insurance) to protect against negligence claims based on mistakes your company made or your company's failure to perform.

Insurance is not a "set it and forget it" item

Because changes in your business often warrant changes in your insurance coverages, annual reviews with your insurance broker are a must. You'll want to discuss the impact of:

- Purchases or sales of assets (including vehicles and equipment)

- Changes in sales volumes

- New products or services offered

- Leases ended or entered into

- Changes in key personnel

- Other significant changes

Learn How to Shop for Business Insurance

EVERY BUSINESS NEEDS A VARIETY of insurance policies. Once you have an understanding of what you need, the next step is to know how to shop for insurance to ensure you get a good price on it all.

Start by doing your homework

Here's what I recommend:

- **Network** – Get to know 5 insurance brokers with solid reputations.

- **Identify carriers** – Determine who the top insurance carriers are in your industry. Find out if your trade association endorses particular carriers.

- **Check coverage requirements** – Make a list of all the insurance coverage requirements in your agreements with customers, suppliers and lenders.

- **Research coverage options** – See what is available for the type of policy you need, and then make a list of "must haves" and "can live withouts." For example, if you're shopping for health insurance for your employees, is a PPO a must, or will an HMO be fine?

- **Improve your metrics** – Premiums are often calculated based on a formula. Find out what this formula is and then gather your historical data that relates to it. See if there's anything you can do to improve your metrics before you start getting bids. Then develop a projection of these metrics for the upcoming policy year based on the formula and any changes you intend to make.

- **Qualify for discounts** – Learn what best practices and procedures need to be in place in order to take advantage of all available discounts. If you're not already doing these things, start doing them now.

- **Avoid surcharges** – With many types of insurance, events that are considered to be outside the norm will result in surcharges. Understand what typically causes surcharges for the type of insurance you're researching and look at ways to avoid them.

Then solicit bids

By this point you should have a thorough understanding of what's out there and what you need, and a projection that includes estimates of the metrics that the insurers need to know.

Reach out to two or three of the brokers on your list and ask for quotes. Be specific in your communications to ensure you'll be able to make "apples to apples" comparisons once the quotes come in— in terms of both the assumptions that the insurer uses to calculate the quote and the specifics of the coverage provided. Evaluate the quotes and move forward!

Control Your Workers' Comp Premiums

WORKERS' COMPENSATION INSURANCE premiums are based on what's known as the "experience mod rate." This is an actuarial number assigned to your company based on your past experience with workers' comp claims.

Here's how the experience mod works. Say the "base rate" for coverage is $100 per month. If your experience mod is 0.75, then your premium will be $75. But if your experience mod is 1.25, you'll pay $125 for the same coverage.

Minimize your claims

The key to low premiums is to have a low experience mod rate, which requires minimizing your claims. This is especially important because your experience mod is based on a multi-year calculation. This means that you'll feel the pain of each claim for years.

Put a solid risk management plan in place

To reduce injuries and workers' comp claims, implement a Risk Management Plan that requires you to:

- **Watch for trends** – Review three years' worth of claims to identify any patterns that emerge. For example, are you seeing a lot of lower back injuries? If so, why? And what can you do to address this problem?

- **Have a written Safety Plan** – If you are in California, this plan must be in compliance with Cal/OSHA requirements, which vary by industry. Your workers' comp broker may be able to provide a template for this.

- **Conduct regular safety training** – Get buy-in by asking employees what the company can do to make the workplace safer for them, and then act on these recommendations.

- **Perform regular safety inspections** – While most office environments can get by with an annual inspection, others (such as construction and manufacturing firms) should inspect their workplace at least once each day.

Be proactive

No one is going to care more about controlling your costs than you will.

- **Get multiple bids** – Be sure to get two or three quotes, preferably from solid companies that will help you with risk management.

- **Manage open claims** – Work with the Claims Manager at your insurance provider to get claims closed as quickly as possible. If a claim is open at year end the insurer will establish a reserve for it. This reserve, which may be several times greater than what has actually been spent on treatment, goes into the calculation of your experience mod...even if it ultimately turns out to be more than actual costs.

- **Pay attention to your insurance classification codes** – Like any form of insurance, premiums for Workers' Compensation insurance are based on risk factors. One of these is the likelihood of injury, which is determined based on the type of work performed. For example, a rodeo clown is more likely to get injured than a telephone operator. The classification codes, which in California are set by the Workers' Compensation Insurance Rating Bureau (WCIRB), reflect this.

  o **Your classification codes are assigned to you.** A representative of the WCRIB will periodically visit your company and do an inspection and audit to determine your classification codes. Be sure they are correct! This will help keep your premiums as low as possible.

  There might be two codes that are very similar, but one will cost you 10% more than the other. Sometimes employees are misclassified in the first place. Other times employees are misclassified because things have changed over time. For example, if you have purchased machinery that reduces the risk of what was being done manually in the past, the classification code might change.

If your codes need to be adjusted, contact the WCIRB and complain loudly enough to convince them to come back out and take another look at your operation. Your insurance broker may be able to help you with this.

o **There is a standard premium rate associated with each code.** Base premiums are calculated by multiplying payroll x classification code x experience mod rate.

o **You must report your payroll in each of your assigned classification codes.** Be sure to report it accurately by avoiding typos and mistakes.

o **You must also provide payroll projections.** Each year your insurance company will require a projection of payroll for the upcoming year, listed by classification code. Your premium will be based on this projection, subject to adjustment after an audit at year-end. Getting these projections right is obviously important.

Be Aware that
You Need EPL Insurance

HARASSMENT. DISCRIMINATION. Wrongful termination. Failure to promote. Infliction of emotional distress. What do all of these things (and more) have in common? They are all situations for which everyone from customers to current, potential and former employees can sue your company.

If you have Employment Practices Liability insurance (EPL),

these situations are all covered risks. But if you don't have Employment Practices Liability insurance, you are essentially "self-insuring," which can be an enormous mistake. Defending your company against employment practices claims can be so expensive that sometimes just a single EPL lawsuit causes a small business to go under completely.

To understand how expensive these claims can be, let's look at some real-life examples, as provided by insurance companies[1]:

- **Age discrimination** – A 62-year-old sales rep filed an age discrimination suit after he was fired for not making his sales quotas. The settlement: $540,000.

- **Sexual harassment and retaliation** – An employee claimed that she faced retaliation after she complained about sexual harassment. Total defense and settlement costs: over $550,000.

- **Emotional distress** – An employee claimed that derogatory statements were posted by co-workers on an online company bulletin board. After the employer denied responsibility, the employee sued for defamation and emotional distress. Total defense and settlement costs: over $600,000.

- **Sexual harassment and retaliation** – After being fired for divulging confidential information, an employee filed a retaliation and sexual harassment suit, claiming the CFO's behavior had been inappropriate for quite some time. Total defense costs: $150,000.

Yes, it *can* happen to you

Think that because you're dedicated to doing things right that this can never happen to you? Think again. One in ten businesses will face an employment practices charge. Which actually seems low given the results of a recent survey, in which 35% of respondents—including 41% of women respondents—stated that they had been harassed at work at some point in their career. [1] Plus, contrary to the #metoo stereotypes, not all harassers are bosses or men. This survey also found that 22% of alleged harassers were women, and 27% were peers.

Two more things to keep in mind: Many employment practices lawsuits are filed by former employees, when it's too late to put an end to the offending behavior. And even handling unfounded allegations takes time and money.

Prevention, early detection, appropriate responses and proper insurance coverage are all key to dealing with Employment Practices Liability issues.

[1] 2018 Hiscox Workplace Harassment Study

Know What's Required Under COBRA

IF YOU OFFER GROUP HEALTH CARE benefits to your employees and their dependents, you must stay in compliance with COBRA, the law that says you have to give individuals who would otherwise lose their coverage the option to continue on your group plan for a specified length of time. Here are some important things about COBRA that you need to know:

- **Who is entitled to COBRA coverage?** COBRA applies to employees whose hours are reduced, or whose employment is terminated for reasons other than gross misconduct. For spouses the qualifying events also include divorce or legal separation, death of the covered employee, or the covered employee becoming entitled to Medicare. For dependent children qualifying events also include losing their dependent child status under the plan rules.

- **What type of coverage do I have to offer under COBRA?** Basically, you must give COBRA participants the same insurance options that you are giving everyone else.

- **How long does COBRA coverage last?** Federal COBRA generally lasts for 18 months. In some situations it can extend to 29 or 36 months.

- **Do I have to pay for or subsidize COBRA coverage?** Generally speaking, no. Although this temporarily changed during the COVID-19 pandemic, in most cases the COBRA recipient is responsible for making the premium payments, which can be 102% of the full cost of the plan.

- **What are my notification duties?** You must provide written notification to covered employees and their covered spouses of their rights when they first join the group health care plan, in the summary plan description, and within a specified period of time when a qualifying event occurs (at which point you must also notify the plan administrator). You also have to maintain records showing that you've done all of this.

- **What if I don't comply with the COBRA notice rules?** In this case, get out your checkbook! The IRS can hit you with a $100 per day or $2,500 per affected beneficiary excise tax (or more). The Department of Labor will levy penalties of $110 per day, per violation. Plus, you can be required to pay for the affected individuals' medical expenses and more.

- **What if I have less than 20 employees?** In this case, Cal-COBRA, the California state law, applies. Cal-COBRA is rather similar to COBRA except it affects employers with two to 20 employees, and mandates that these employees be given the option to continue coverage for 36 months. Under Cal-COBRA, individuals who have used up their 18 months of federal COBRA can get an additional 18 months, for a combined period of 36 months.

Take a Close Look at D&O Insurance

THERE'S NOTHING LIKE BEING SLAPPED with a lawsuit to make a business' management team wish they had proper insurance in place. For smaller businesses, Directors and Officers Insurance ("D&O Insurance") often falls into this category, as they mistakenly believe it's not something they need.

D&O insurance covers managers, too

However, D&O insurance is for companies of all sizes because it helps protect the company's managers, directors and officers from lawsuits claiming that they have acted wrongfully. It provides liability coverage for claims based on the impact of the decisions and actions (or lack of action) these people have taken within the scope of their regular duties.

Although a lot of people will refuse to serve on a Board of Directors if the company doesn't have D&O insurance in place, many managerial employees do not realize that they can be *personally* sued for their actions as well. But the reality is, a claimant might not just go after your company's "deep pockets." Individuals within your company (including the owner) can be sued, too.

What happens if you don't have D&O insurance?

D&O insurance protects the personal assets of your company's managers and corporate directors and officers, plus all of their spouses, if they should be personally sued by employees, vendors, competitors, customers, investors or other parties, for actual or alleged wrongful acts committed in the course of managing the company.

Like any insurance policy, if you never have a lawsuit or claim, nothing happens.

But if you do need it, you're glad you have it! For example, Chubb's 2018 Private Company Risk Survey found that 26% of private companies reported experiencing a D&O loss in the last three years, with the average reported loss being a whopping $399,394.

If you can easily afford a $399K (or more) loss, go ahead and "self-insure." Otherwise, not having this can be catastrophic.

What types of things are covered by D&O insurance?

D&O coverage applies to a wide variety of situations in which the directors, managers and officers of a company might be held personally liable for a negative outcome. This includes claims related to:

- **Negligent management**

- **Breaches of fiduciary duty**

- **Employment**

- **Breaches of contract**

- **Relationships with creditors**

- **Regulatory issues**

- **Inadequate disclosures on financial statements**

- **And more**

Don't let a lack of insurance bring your company down

Yes, like all insurance policies, D&O coverage is not free. But is it worth the money? Any company that has actually faced a D&O claim would say "yes."

Chapter 7:
Human Resources

"Clients do not come first. Employees come first.
If you take care of your employees,
they will take care of the clients."

~ Richard Branson

Put Strong
Written HR Policies in Place

I HAVE OFTEN HEARD OWNERS of small businesses say that their firm is too small to need written human resources (HR) policies. After all, their three employees are all "like family," so the formality of written rules and regulations seems a bit absurd. Until, that is, something that an employee handbook could have enabled them to avoid goes wrong, and they pay the price for their laxness in terms of lawsuits, fines, morale problems and more.

The reality is, *every* employer should have written HR policies in place. These policies clearly communicate the benefits that the company offers, and clearly communicate rules and expectations to everyone so that they can be enforced evenly and fairly. They help protect the employer from employment-related lawsuits and help ensure compliance with governmental regulations. In short, they're a good idea.

How to create written HR policies

Luckily, getting a basic employee handbook in place is easier than you might think. The key is to avoid starting from scratch. There are a wide variety of customizable employee handbook templates and creation tools available online. Your trade association may have one as well. Just be sure to choose a template that is in compliance with the latest labor laws and appropriate for the specifics of your industry and state.

What should your employee handbook include?

While the following is not an exhaustive list, at a minimum your employee handbook should include:

- **A brief explanation** of what your company does, including your vision and mission.

- **Standards of acceptable behavior**, such as policies regarding work hours, breaks, overtime, dress code, absences and substance abuse.

- **Safety-related rules**, especially those needed to comply with OSHA or other regulations.

- **Anti-harassment policies** (including sexual harassment), the process for lodging a complaint, and your process for responding to complaints.

- **Rules regulating the use of electronics**, including company computers, personal cell phones, internet access and more.

- **Consequences for breaking the rules**. What warrants immediate firing? What is your discipline process?

- **Company-paid benefits**, including holidays, vacations, sick pay, family medical leave, medical insurance, etc. For paid time off you should explain how the benefit is calculated and the process for scheduling and taking it.

- **Policies regarding performance reviews**.

Prevent Unauthorized Overtime

WHAT HAPPENS WHEN ONE OF YOUR non-exempt employees works unauthorized overtime—even if you had expressly forbidden this person from putting in the extra time? If you are in California, you have to pay them for this forbidden overtime (at overtime rates) anyway! California law clearly states that you must pay hourly workers for *all* time worked. Obviously, this is not a desirable situation.

Here are some ideas for how to stop your employees from working unauthorized overtime:

- **Have a strong written overtime policy in place** – Your Employee Manual should include a formal policy stating that employees may not punch in early or punch out late without prior written authorization from their supervisor. Back this policy up with strong progressive discipline consequences. Make it clear that continuing to work overtime after being instructed not to can be considered insubordination, and employees who work unauthorized overtime can be written up, suspended or even terminated.

- **Enforce your policy** – Review time sheets daily and implement your disciplinary procedures in every unauthorized overtime situation.

- **Keep everyone aware of the policy** – Regularly remind your hourly employees and their supervisors that ALL overtime

MUST be signed off by the supervisor on the day it is worked.

- **Educate your supervisors** – Your supervisors must understand their role in enforcing your overtime policies, as well as the laws stating that non-exempt employees must be paid for all time worked. Once the time has been worked, the supervisor cannot tell the employee not to report it and cannot refuse to authorize payment for those hours.

- **Hold supervisors accountable** – Your policy should include disciplinary consequences for supervisors who fail to take action to implement your overtime policies.

- **Turn off their computers** – If your non-exempt employees require the use of a computer to do their jobs, another option is to have your IT department automatically shut down these employees' computers at a specific time each day.

Hire the Right Person

IT HAPPENS ALL THE TIME. A person who is viewed as an important part of the team leaves the company, and in their rush to fill the vacancy, management settles for someone who is not a good fit. Then that wrong person causes problems, and the company ends up worse off than if they had left the position vacant.

The reality is, it's a bad idea to rush the hiring process. To ensure that you hire the right person for the job, here are some of the steps that should not be skipped:

- **Update the job description** – Talk to the department heads with whom this person will interact. Identify the job duties, the skill sets required to perform those job duties and the soft skills necessary to succeed in the position.

  In addition, be sure your written job description includes the physical abilities that are genuinely necessary to perform the job duties. I recently heard of a company that hired a security guard who managed to hide the fact that he was legally blind. By the time the company found out, it was too late. Since the job description didn't mention the ability to see, they could not fire him without running afoul of employment laws!

- **Have a fair wage scale** – Your pay structure needs to be generous enough to attract quality people.

- **Ask good questions during the interview** – Your questions should enable you to evaluate if the person has both the job skills and the soft skills that you're looking for.

- **Check references** – Verify that the statements on the candidate's application are all true.

- **Listen to your gut** – If someone looks great on paper but is really rubbing you the wrong way, or if there seems to be a big disconnect between who they are on paper and who they are in person, recognize this as a "red flag."

- **Take advantage of the probationary period** – Make sure your company has a clear written policy regarding the 90-day "probationary period." During this time evaluate the new hire every 30 days. This way you can give them an opportunity to improve and will build a case for quickly letting them go if they are clearly not working out.

If your company, like most, is running with a lean staff, you just can't afford to settle for mediocrity. Good hires are productive. Bad hires are counterproductive, and it can be difficult to fire someone once they've come on board.

Let the State Chip in for Your Training Program

ALTHOUGH FEW COMPANIES ARE AWARE OF IT, California has a program dedicated to reimbursing employers for the costs associated with providing job skills training to their employees. In fact, each year California's Employment Training Panel (ETP) awards millions of dollars to qualifying companies!

The money comes from taxes levied on California businesses, including the $7 per employee that you, as a California employer, pay into the fund each year.

Here's what you need to know about ETP funding...

What types of companies qualify?

While a broad spectrum of California employers can qualify, at times the ETP has given priority to those in the following industries:

- Agriculture
- Biotechnology and Life Sciences
- Construction

- Green Technology
- Information Technology Services
- Manufacturing
- Multimedia and Entertainment
- Nursing and Healthcare
- Transportation Logistics

Is this available for small businesses?

Technically yes, but from a practical standpoint this is best for businesses that have at least 40 employees.

How much can you get?

The answer depends on a variety of factors, but we're talking real money here! Plus, these awards are actual checks in the mail— not tax credits. For example, February 2021 awards included $2,000 per trainee for a manufacturing company and $1,242 per trainee for a biotech company; December 2020 awards included $1,380 per trainee for a healthcare provider and $529 per trainee to teach business skills to employees of a dairy farm.

What sort of training qualifies?

Pretty much anything other than legally-mandated courses. So while it won't reimburse you for your sexual harassment prevention training class, everything from computer skills and business skills to machinery operation, estimating, scheduling and a whole lot more is eligible.

Who delivers the training?

You're responsible for the actual training. Either you design and deliver it, or you hire a third party to do so. Basically, this is "free money" to help pay for the training you're doing anyway.

The bottom line is, ETP funding can be a significant competitive advantage for your firm. The only catch is that, being a government program, there are a lot of hoops to jump through to get the money. Rather than deal with the steep learning curve, though, most companies simply hire specialists to take care of the paperwork for them.

Understand When Salespeople Get Overtime Pay

CALIFORNIA HAS VERY STRINGENT guidelines regarding which of your workers are "exempt" or "non-exempt" from overtime wage rules—and getting it wrong can be very costly. One misclassification can trigger multiple wage violations and their associated monetary penalties!

What I've seen is that the question of whether salespeople are exempt or non-exempt often trips employers up. Which is no surprise, since the answer is different for "outside salespeople" than it is "inside salespeople"—and the state has specific definitions for each of these categories. Here's what you need to know...

Most (but not all) inside salespeople are non-exempt

In most situations inside salespeople are entitled to overtime pay. However, inside salespeople who meet *all* of the following criteria are exempt from overtime pay:

- Work in an industry governed by Wage Order Number 4 or 7;

- Are primarily engaged in sales;

- Have earnings that exceed 1.5 times the minimum wage for each hour worked during the pay period; and

- Receive more than half of their earnings each pay period from commissions.

Most (but not all) outside salespeople are exempt

In determining if a worker meets the "outside salesperson" exemption, look at their actual job duties and not just their job title. This is because California law defines an "outside salesperson" as someone who:

- Is at least 18 years old;

- Spends at least 50% of their time in the field, working away from their employer's place of business (which can be a home office, company worksite or other designated physical worksite); and

- Spends at least 50% of their time selling products or services, or obtaining orders or contracts for the sale of products or services.

Be aware that while time spent traveling to and from sales appointments counts as "time spent selling," time spent doing pretty much anything else, including delivering merchandise that was previously purchased, does not count as time spent selling.

In addition, the "50% in the field" criteria means that if your outside salesperson spends more time sitting at their desk making phone calls than they do going out and meeting with people face-to-face, the state says you must classify them as an inside salesperson. In this case, the "inside salesperson" criteria must be used to determine exempt vs. non-exempt status.

Chapter 8:
The Role of the CFO

"The successful CFO makes people comfortable by inspiring trust."

~ Samuel Dergel

Recognize What a CFO Can Do for Your Business

MUCH MORE THAN "JUST" a "numbers person," a CFO is a businessperson with many skills—including the ability to analyze your numbers and help you make informed decisions based on this data. If your business is growing, you don't have to wait until you need a full-time CFO to start reaping the benefits of a CFO's expertise. You can bring in a part-time CFO like me right now!

Even working on only a part-time basis, there's a lot that a CFO can do that will have a significant impact on your business' success. This includes:

- **Develop a strategic plan, goals and budgets** – What are your goals for the next 12 months? Does your management team have a workable plan to make them happen, or is everyone just showing up and hoping for the best?

  A CFO can work with senior management to create a comprehensive strategic plan, as well as goals for this year and the next four years. Then create a detailed budget based on these plans and goals.

- **Analyze all the numbers** – Look at the trends, review profitability by service or product line, monitor the budget and more. Analyze your firm's overall financial health and provide expert advice as to where to go from here.

- **Help you understand if you're adding value to your company** – Are your financial ratios improving? If so, you may be able to get better interest rates, larger credit limits on your trade payables and more money when you sell the company.

- **Maintain your banking relationships** – Help you obtain necessary financing, and then ensure all loan reporting requirements are met.

- **Analyze and strengthen your customer base** – As I discussed in a previous tip, some customers bring a lot more to your bottom line than others. Take a close look at your margins by customer, especially your largest volume customers. Take steps to up-sell higher-margin products to your lower-margin customers. Reduce customer-caused fire drills overall. And consider firing your least profitable customers.

- **Ensure you're getting the best prices** – Are you getting the best prices from all of your vendors? When was the last time you got competitive quotes on your top 10 spending line items aside from labor? And speaking of labor, do you participate in industry wage studies, such as those done by your trade association? Are you paying a competitive wage? Are you paying too much for your brother-in-law, or about to lose a great employee because you're paying less than the going rate?

- **Supervise the Accounting, HR and IT Departments** – Plus work with department heads to identify areas for improvement and implement trackable solutions for these issues.

- **Improve your accounting processes** – Help your senior accounting personnel expedite the month-end close to ensure you get accurate and timely financial statements. Create easy-to-use dashboards that give you real-time financial data for effectively managing your business. Develop a template to also capture the information that lenders require.

- **Identify and eliminate wasteful spending** – See where your money is going, including right-sizing the Accounting Department. This also often involves looking at your "miscellaneous" expense category, which is usually either money that should not have been spent, or things that only benefit the executives. Sometimes it's the owner's "slush fund" – but the owner has no idea where the money is going.

- **Provide valuable introductions** – Bring in already-vetted professionals as needed, such as lawyers, CPAs, insurance brokers and marketing experts.

The bottom line is, an experienced CFO can make a significant difference for your bottom line!

Find the Right Part-Time CFO For Your Business

YOU'RE READY TO BRING IN A PART-TIME CFO. Now what? What should you look at when evaluating candidates for the job?

Start with your specific needs

Chances are the majority of your part-time CFO's

responsibilities will be project-based. A logical starting point is therefore to take a close look at what you expect this person to accomplish. List the three biggest projects for which you need help, and then seek a CFO with experience addressing these types of issues.

Consider some consulting-related factors

Your part-time CFO will most likely be a 1099'd outside consultant. As such, you'll want to find out:

- **How quickly can they get up to speed?** You want someone who can come in and hit the ground running. Do they have the background and expertise to pull this off?

- **What is their availability?** Can they offer you the hours and flexibility you need going forward?

- **What resources do they bring?** If a project gets too big, or if you need help from professionals in other fields, do they have a network of vetted experts they can tap?

Then look at experience and qualifications in general

Of course, in many ways hiring a part-time CFO is similar to hiring a full-time CFO. You'll also want to consider all of the usual hiring factors, such as:

- **Education, credentials, experience & track record** – Be sure to look at the specifics here. Do they have a CPA? Do they appear to have the ability to understand your business? Do they have experience doing the broad array of things that you will ultimately need, or just a subset of this? For example, some

CFOs are great with strategic planning but not well-versed in insurance-related issues. If you need both, this person would not be a good match.

- **Communication & interpersonal skills** – Will they be able to analyze the numbers and then communicate useful, actionable information to you based on what they find?

- **Management style** – As a part-time CFO, how will they fit in with both your management team and the staff members that they'll supervise and/or work with?

- **Personal chemistry** – You'll be working very closely with this person, and they'll be working with the intimate details of your business. It's got to be a good fit!

The right part-time CFO can make a big difference for your company. Before hiring someone, be sure to complete a thorough interview process, check references and do a background check.

Hire the Right Full-Time CFO For Your Business

YOUR BUSINESS IS GROWING, and week after week you're finding yourself asking your part-time CFO to put in extra hours. It's time to make the leap to a full-time CFO! Here are some key things you should look for when hiring for this critically-important role:

- **Industry expertise** – While a good CFO's skill set should enable this person to transition from industry to industry, the reality is that many industries have unique needs. Look for someone who either already understands yours or is willing to take on the challenge of learning all about it.

- **Education and background** – Do they have a CPA? Are they experienced in all or most of the things you will need them to do, or just a subset of this? For example, you may need your CFO to do more than manage the financial aspects of the business; the CFO is often the one who oversees IT and Human Resources as well. Which means you're looking for someone with a strong enough understanding of these areas to be able to hire and manage the right people...and the energy to do so.

- **Ability to manage change** – In a growing company the CFO is often called upon to help get everyone on board with changes that need to happen, and then manage the change process as it takes place. Look for a CFO who has successfully done this in the past.

- **Problem solving abilities** – Ask the job candidate about their top accomplishments in the past five years. Their answers will likely shed some light on their problem-solving skills, as well as their willingness to tackle new challenges and learn new things.

- **Soft skills** – As with all new hires, excellent communication and interpersonal skills are vital. Once they crunch the numbers, for example, will they be able to communicate useful, actionable information to you based on their findings? Will their management style fit in with your company culture? Will they contribute valuable viewpoints and expertise to the management team?

- **Computer skills** – At most companies, the CFO will need to be current in Microsoft Office products, including Excel, PowerPoint and Word...and how all of this works in the Cloud with Office 365.

The right CFO can make a big difference for your company. Unfortunately, as some of my clients have learned the hard way, the wrong CFO can make a big difference, too—through bad advice, shoddy work or even outright criminal activity, such as embezzlement. The lesson here is you must take the time to find and hire the right person. Don't just fill the seat!

Chapter 9:
Business Succession

*"One of the things we often miss in succession planning
is that it should be gradual and thoughtful...
so that it's almost a non-event when it happens."*

~ Anne M. Mulcahy

Position Your Company to Sell for Maximum Value

CONSIDERING SELLING YOUR BUSINESS? The time to start building value is long before you put the company on the market. To position your company so it will sell at the highest price, here are some of the things you should do:

- **Assemble a strong management team** – What I often see in small businesses is that the owner or CEO is the "face" of the company and, in effect, its only intangible asset. To sell the company you need to have a strong management team in place that customers and vendors are comfortable doing business with.

  Make yourself less important. Give your managers authority to make decisions, and ensure that customers, vendors and other outsiders have a chance to get to know them. Help your managers develop strong reputations within your industry, such as by joining and participating in your trade association.

- **Retain key employees** – A deferred compensation plan can encourage key employees to stick around after a sale.

- **Get your operations in top shape** – This includes having strong financial controls and appropriate policies and procedures in place, strengthening your customer base, and more.

- **Acquire strong vendor contracts** – This is especially important if you're a reseller. Can you get advantageous pricing and/or terms? Would they be willing to grant territorial exclusivity?

- **Increase earnings** – When you provide potential buyers with historical data, you'll want the sales and expenses reflected in that data to look good.

  Keep in mind that when talking about maximizing profitability, most people generally think that increasing sales volume is the answer. This is not always the case. Sometimes a better approach is to shrink the company. A smaller company can narrow its focus to just providing the services or products that can be sold at the highest gross margins.

- **Create 5 years of adjusted historical financial records** – Start by identifying any unusual or non-recurring expenses that can be added back in. The goal is to show what the true results of operation would have been if the company had been run "by the books" and didn't have these unusual transactions.

  For example, if you own both the company and the facility in which it operates, and you have a sweetheart rental agreement that gives you above-market rents, you should adjust the records as though only market rate was paid. Or if you've been paying high salaries to family members who aren't really providing services, adjust the records to remove them from the payroll.

- **Create a 3- to 5-year business plan with projected financials** – Include a narrative of what you expect to happen and the resources that will be needed to get there. Be sure your projected cash flow statement ties to your projected income statement and balance sheet.

One thing to keep in mind here is that a business' selling price is often determined by a multiple of expected cash flow. Pay close attention to this and look at steps you can take now to increase your cash position.

Don't wait until you have an interested potential buyer to start getting your ducks in a row.

About Don Welker

AFTER GAINING OVER 30 YEARS of experience as a financial executive at private firms in and "Big 4" public accounting serving both privately-owned and publicly-held firms, Don Welker now works as a part-time CFO, bringing his extensive expertise to growing Southern California businesses.

As a seasoned CFO, Don is known for his extensive financial management expertise, experience with a broad array of industries, excellent communication skills, and ethics, dependability and resourcefulness.

For information about how Don can help your company, visit www.DonWelker.com or contact Don directly at 951.533.4966 or Don@DonWelker.com.

Made in the USA
Columbia, SC
30 October 2021